The Dog Lover's Coffee-Table Book

Written and compiled by

Nanette Newman and Graham Tarrant

Drawings by Edward McLachlan

COLLINS
St James's Place, London
1982

Newman, Nanette
   The dog lover's coffee-table book.
   1. Dogs—Anecdotes, facetiae, satire, etc.
   I. Title   II. Tarrant, Graham
   636.7   SF426.5

   ISBN 0-00-216463-9

William Collins Sons & Co Ltd
London · Glasgow · Sydney · Auckland
Toronto · Johannesburg

First published 1982
© in the text Bryan Forbes Limited and Graham Tarrant 1982
© in the illustrations Edward McLachlan 1982
Cover photograph of authors by John Rogers

ISBN 0 00 216463 9

Photoset in Baskerville
Made and Printed in Great Britain by
Wm Collins Sons & Co Ltd Glasgow

INTRODUCTION

As coffee-table books go, this is a bit on the small side. There's not much in the way of glossy colour pictures either. On the other hand, how many coffee-table books can you pop into your pocket to read in the launderette; or lift up in bed without breaking both wrists; or get your dog to carry in its mouth when you take it for a walk? And as coffee-table books go, it's amazingly cheap.

Like dogs themselves (not to mention dog lovers), the pieces in the book are a rather odd assortment: funny, fascinating, sad, charming, bizarre or quite simply mind-blowing. All, hopefully, are entertaining and provide further proof, if proof is needed, of the very special relationship that exists between *them* and *us*.

Incidentally, you don't have to wait until you get the book home before you start dipping into it – which makes it an *instant* coffee-table book.

NANETTE NEWMAN
GRAHAM TARRANT

For Ros and Bryan

DOG, n. A kind of additional or subsidiary Deity designed to catch the overflow and surplus of the world's worship. This Divine Being in some of his smaller and silkier incarnations takes, in the affection of Woman, the place to which there is no human male aspirant. The Dog is a survival – an anachronism. He toils not, neither does he spin, yet Solomon in all his glory never lay upon a door-mat all day long, sun-soaked and fly-fed and fat, while his master worked for the means wherewith to purchase an idle wag of the Solomonic tail, seasoned with a look of tolerant recognition.

The Devil's Dictionary by Ambrose Bierce

Wrong make of dog

A Bath man who was in his local pub one weekend suddenly realized that his dog was missing. He hurried out and was anxiously looking around the car park when he was hailed by an elderly woman in a parked Mini, who asked him if he had lost something.

'Yes, my Dobermann,' he replied.

'Oh dear,' the woman said, 'did you leave the keys in it?'

Daily Telegraph

Seen outside a house in Bucks County, Pennsylvania:

BEWARE OF THE DOG
SURVIVORS WILL BE PROSECUTED

I loathe people who keep dogs. They are cowards who haven't got the guts to bite people themselves.

August Strindberg

KEEP OFF THE PAGE

When some of James Thurber's famous dog drawings appeared in the *American*, the owner of the newspaper, William Randolph Hearst, sent a message to the editor: 'STOP RUNNING THOSE DOGS ON YOUR PAGE. I WOULDN'T HAVE THEM PEEING ON MY CHEAPEST RUG.'

The dog has got more fun out of man
than man has got out of the dog,
for man is the more laughable of the two animals.

James Thurber

CHICKEN AND THE EGG

Bob is a fine two-year-old mastiff, with head and face of massive strength, heightened by great mildness of expression. One day he was seen carrying a hen very gently in his mouth to the kennel. Placing her in one corner, he stood sentry while she laid an egg, which he at once devoured. From that day the two have been fast friends, the hen refusing to lay anywhere but in Bob's kennel, and getting her reward in the dainty morsels from his platter. There must have been a bit of canine reasoning here. Bob must have found eggs to his liking, learnt that they were laid by hens, and that he could best secure a supply by having a hen to himself.

Spectator, 7 July 1888

The dog's kennel is not the place to keep a sausage.
Danish proverb

THE MORTGAGE LIFTER

Rin Tin Tin, who became one of the biggest box office attractions of the silent screen, was one of a litter of puppies found abandoned in a German dugout during World War I. In a career spanning fifty films, this amazing dog earned more than a million dollars as well as the nickname 'the mortgage lifter' – so called because it was mainly the revenue from his films that held off the studio's creditors in the lean years.

Rin Tin Tin had his own valet and chef, together with a private limousine and chauffeur. He was insured for one hundred thousand dollars, although his movie stunts weren't always as dangerous as they looked. The countless windowpanes he crashed through, with great dramatic effect, were made of translucent candy.

When making silent films, Rin Tin Tin's master, Lee Duncan, would call out instructions to the dog on the set. But the advent of the Talkies made this impossible, and some other way of directing him had to be found. The problem was finally solved by some children's toys, among them a black velvet cat, a stuffed lion, and a small woollen rabbit. When confronted with the cat Rin Tin Tin would go into a rage; the lion caused him to bark incessantly; whilst the sight of the woolly rabbit would be sure to bring a smile to the dog's face and a wag to his tail.

Like other Hollywood celebrities, Rin Tin Tin had a home in Beverly Hills. He also had a beautiful wife called Nannette, who bore him four sons that carried on in the business. In 1932, at the age of fourteen, Rin Tin Tin collapsed and died in the arms of his neighbour Jean Harlow – appropriately playing his final scene opposite another of the cinema's greatest names.

Hounded by the Law

A visitor to Dijon, in
France, in August 1764,
related this strange tale in
a letter to a friend in
London. It was later published
in *The Scots Magazine*.

Since my arrival here there has been a
man broke on the wheel, with no other
proof to condemn him than that of a
water spaniel about the size of yours.
The circumstances attending it being so
very singular and striking, I beg leave
to communicate them to you.

A farmer who had been to
receive a sum of money,
was waylaid, robbed
and murdered by two
villains. The farmer's
dog returned with all speed to the
gentleman's house who had paid the
money, and expressed such amazing
anxiety for the gentleman to follow him,
pulling him several times by the sleeve
and skirt of the coat, that at length the
gentleman submitted. The dog led him

to a field, a little from the road-side, where the body lay. From thence the gentleman went to a public-house, in order to alarm the country. The moment he entered (as the two villains were there drinking) the dog seized the murderer by the throat and the other made his escape. This man lay in prison three months, during which time they visited him once a week with the dog; and though they made him change his clothes with other prisoners, and always stand in the midst of a crowd, yet would the dog find him out, and always fly at him. On the day of trial, when the prisoner was at the bar, the dog was let loose in the court-house and in the midst of some hundreds he always found him out (though in entirely new clothes) and would have tore him to pieces, had he been allowed. In consequence of which, he was condemned; and at the place of execution he confessed the fact. Surely so useful, so disinterestedly faithful an animal should not be so barbarously treated as I have seen them, particularly in London.

MAIL-BITING

Each year more than 4000 British postmen are bitten by dogs, with twenty per cent of them off work for at least three days as a result of their injuries.

The Post Office procedure following an assault is to send an official letter of complaint to the owner of the dog in question – which, of course, has to be delivered by the postman.

DOG DETECTIVE

When the wealthy inhabitants of Beverly Hills, home of the stars, lose a dog, they send for Sherlock Bones, the dog detective. Sherlock and his canine assistant, who sports a deerstalker hat, search the neighbourhood for the missing animal and advise the owner on how big a reward to offer. The dog detective claims a seventy per cent success rate – which makes him quite a retriever.

A man out alone on the moor
Could hardly believe what he saw
Coming out of the bog
Was a massive black dog
With a Sherlock Holmes hat in his jaw.

Insertion Rate

The following advertisement appeared in *The Dog Times* on 18 May 1906.

STUD DOGS.

- - TARIFF - -

				per inch
For One Insertion	...	...	...	4/-
For One to Six Insertions (each insertion)...				3/9
For Thirteen	,,	,,	...	3/6
For Twenty-six	,,	,,	...	3/-
For Fifty-two	,,	,,	...	2/6

Dog Collars

The following items were listed in an inventory of furniture to be found in the palaces of Henry VIII in 1419:

Two Greyhoundes collars of crimson velvett and cloth of gold, lacking torrettes.

Two other collars with the king's armes, and at the ende portcullis and rose.

Item a collar embroidered with pomegranates and roses with turrets of silver and gilte.

A collar garnished with stole-work with one shallop shelle of silver and gilte, with torrettes and pendauntes of silver and gilte.

A collar of white velvette, embrawdered with perles, the swivels of silver.

Frederick the Great used to carry a small Italian greyhound inside his overcoat when on his military campaigns. And the sixteenth-century French King Henry III liked to walk the streets of Paris with a basket of puppies round his neck.

Royal Dorgies

The kings and queens of England have always surrounded themselves with dogs, and the current monarch is no exception. At the Sandringham Kennels, labradors are bred as gun dogs and for work on the estate. Several have become Field Trial Champions. But there is no doubt that the Court favourites are the corgis.

The first Royal corgi was bought by King George VI (when Duke of York) in 1933. Others soon followed. On her eighteenth birthday, in 1944, Princess Elizabeth was given a corgi of her own: a bitch called Susan. There have been nine generations since then.
The Queen looks after her own dogs as much as possible and they move from house to house with her, living in the private apartments. When they die, they are buried in the grounds of whichever house Her Majesty is residing in at the time.
Three of the longest living corgis – Susan, Sugar and Heather – have their gravestones side by side at Sandringham.

On a number of occasions the Queen has mated a corgi bitch with Princess Margaret's dachshund Pipkin. The result is known in Court circles as a 'Royal Dorgi'.

HAIR OF THE DOG

The Irish poet Thomas Moore recorded the following incident in his diary for 3 June 1827:

Drury had some dogs (two, I believe) sent him that had belonged to Lord Byron. One day he was told that two ladies wished to see him, and he found their business was to ask, as a great favour, some relic of Lord Byron. Expecting to be asked for some of his handwriting, or a bit of his hair, he was amused to find that it was a bit of the hair of one of the dogs they wanted. The dog being brought forward the ladies observed a *clot* on his back, which had evidently resisted any efforts at ablution that might have been exerted on the animal, and immediately selected this as the most precious part to be cut off; 'the probability,' they said, 'being that Lord B. might have patted that clot.'

Alas, poor Prim
I'm sorry for him;
I'd rather by half
It had been Sir Ralph.*

Lord Byron on the death of
his wife's toy spaniel.

* Sir Ralph Milbanke, Byron's father-in-law.

BLIND MAN'S BLUFF

Showbiz agent and raconteur Harvey Orkin was standing on Fifth Avenue in New York with a lady friend one afternoon, trying to hail a taxi. It was pouring with rain and there were no cabs about, so they decided to take a bus.

The lady had a Pekinese with her, but the driver of the first bus which came along wouldn't let them on, saying that no dogs were allowed. While they were waiting for the next bus, Orkin went into a nearby shop and bought a white stick and dark glasses. When the bus arrived he groped his way on board, posing as a blind man with a Pekinese guide dog.

'Just a minute,' said the driver, 'I thought all guide dogs were German Shepherds.'

'You mean, he isn't?' Orkin replied.

Achtung!
Achtung!

Cat Killer

From the diary of Samuel Pepys, 11 September 1661:

*To Dr Williams, who did carry me into his garden,
where he hath an abundance of grapes: and he did
show me how a dog that he hath do kill all the cats
that come thither to kill his pigeons, and do afterwards
bury them; and do it with so much care that they shall
be quite covered; that if the tip of the tail hangs out, he
will take up the cat again, and dig the hole deeper,
which is very strange; and he tells me, that he do
believe he hath killed above 100 cats.*

THE WORLD'S RICHEST DOG

When the eccentric American millionairess, Ella Wendel, died in 1931, she left her pet poodle Toby her entire fortune of $30,000,000. Following her death many claimants to the vast estate came forward, and shortly afterwards Toby was destroyed on the order of the executors. The reason given was 'senile decay'.

During Miss Wendel's lifetime, Toby had thousands of dollars lavished upon him. He lived in a room of his own, and had silk cushions and priceless linen to lie on. Each morning his mistress brought him his breakfast in bed, and a butler was specially employed to wait on him.

Ella Wendel's death was the tragedy of Toby's life. He wandered inconsolably through the dark, empty house looking for his beloved mistress. He was made to sleep in a plain basket in the kitchen, and eat his food like any ordinary dog from a bowl. This riches-to-rags story was too much for the millionaire dog. Had he not been put down, he would have expired from a broken heart.

You will find that the woman who is really kind to dogs
is always one who has failed to inspire sympathy in men.

MAX BEERBOHM

Turning Off The Heat

In 1903 Baron and Baroness von Heyden of Holstein, in Germany, patented their invention of a chastity belt for bitches on heat:

> *The von Heydens' New and Improved Means for Preventing Coition* comprises a guard or shield of plaited leather or the like supported by straps and is designed to be worn by bitches and other female animals during the oestrum to prevent cross breeding. It will be found particularly useful in connection with sporting animals and supersedes both the chemical means used heretofore, which are in most cases so injurious as to remedy the animals permanently sterile, and the undesirable practice of isolating the animals during time of rut, which is also exceedingly destructive to their health.

DOG FASHION

Californian dogs are probably the best dressed in the world; certainly the most dressed. Trade is booming for the dozens of pet shops and doggy boutiques, which cater for a wide range of tastes, off the peg or custom-made. T-shirts and sweaters, pyjamas and nighties, raincoats and hats, are in greatest demand; but for the more frivolous there are sailor suits, tu-tus, split-crutch hot pants, and Santa Claus outfits – the last a strictly seasonal item.

And for those who want their pooches to look kosher on the Sabbath, there are *yarmulkes* (skull caps) to fit any head from a Great Dane's to a chihuahua's.

FOURTH TIME UNLUCKY

One of the most poignant dog stories of all time was uncovered with the excavation of Pompeii in the nineteenth century. Among the debris of the ruined city, which had remained buried since the massive eruption of Mount Vesuvius in AD 79, was found the body of a small boy – and alongside it, that of a large dog. Inscribed in Latin on the dog's bronze collar was the following message: 'This dog has three times saved his little master: once from fire, once from drowning, once from thieves.'

The Essenes, an ancient Jewish sect, worshipped dogs. According to their beliefs, there was a King Dog who died at the time of Christ's Crucifixion. And another King Dog will appear to mankind at the end of Christ's thousand-year reign, along with the Kingdom of Heaven.

How odd that people of sense should find any pleasure in being accompanied by a beast who is always spoiling conversation.

Lord Macaulay

A Real Pro

The screen's most versatile acting dog was Teddy, a Great Dane who worked for Mack Sennett, the king of comedy. In one remarkable routine, filmed entirely without a break, Teddy opened a kitchen door, lit the stove with a match held between his teeth, filled a kettle at the sink, put it on the stove, and then, picking up a broom, swept the floor. He could play comedy or drama with equal ease, never missed a cue, and his phenomenal memory put many a two-legged co-star to shame.

Teddy became so valuable to the Sennett studio that a double was hired to perform his more dangerous stunts. And so as not to waste the time of such an important star, a stand-in was used when setting up the camera.

But the smartest thing Teddy ever did was to sign his own contract, for forty dollars a week. In the 1920s, bread like that bought a lot of biscuits.

READ ALL ABOUT IT

Charles A. Dana's famous maxim, 'When a dog bites a man that is not news, but when a man bites a dog that is news', came true in 1960 when Laddy, a police Alsatian, was attacked and bitten on the neck by a man being questioned at Harrow Road police station, in London. The next day the man was sentenced in court to six months imprisonment for assault.

BITTEN BY LION

In his memoirs, *Praeterita*, published in 1899, the critic John Ruskin recalls an incident which took place when he was five years old.

> After one of our long summer journeys my first thought on getting home was to go to see Lion*. My mother trusted me to go to the stable with our one serving-man, Thomas, giving him strict orders that I was not to be allowed within stretch of the dog's chain. Thomas, for better security, carried me in his arms. Lion was at his dinner, and took no notice of either of us; on which I besought leave to pat him. Foolish Thomas stooped towards him that I might, when the dog instantly flew at me, and bit a piece clean out of the corner of my lip on the left side. I was brought up the back stairs, bleeding fast, but not a whit frightened, except lest Lion should be sent away. Lion indeed had to go; but not Thomas: my mother was sure he was sorry, and I think blamed herself the most. The bitten side of the (then really pretty) mouth, was spoiled for evermore, but the wound, drawn close, healed quickly . . . Not the slightest diminution of my love of dogs, nor the slightest nervousness in managing them, was induced by the accident.

* A black Newfoundland.

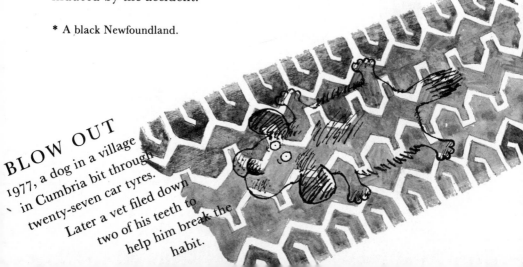

BLOW OUT

1977, a dog in a village in Cumbria bit through twenty-seven car tyres. Later a vet filed down two of his teeth to help him break the habit.

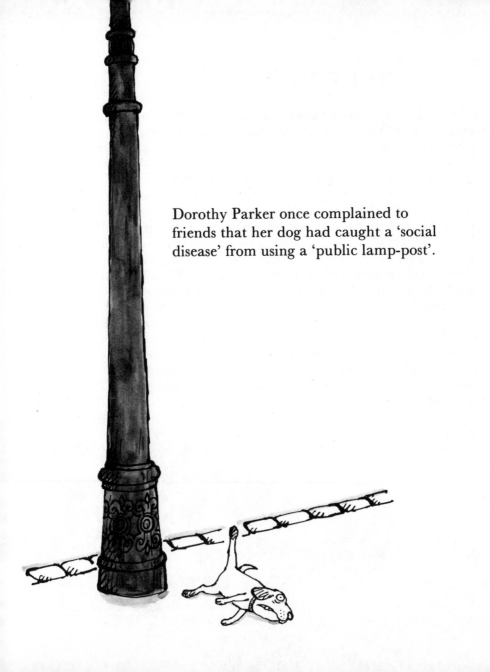

Dorothy Parker once complained to friends that her dog had caught a 'social disease' from using a 'public lamp-post'.

A dog teaches a boy fidelity, perseverance, and to turn around three times before lying down.

ST BARRY

During his distinguished lifetime (1800–14), Barry, a St Bernard, saved forty people from a frozen death on the snow-covered slopes of the Swiss Alps. Time and again, he managed to locate travellers buried beneath the snow after an avalanche, and lead the monks of the Hospice of St Bernard to them.

A contemporary report describes how Barry 'found a child in a frozen state between the bridge of Drouaz and the Ice house of Balsora. He immediately began to lick him, and having succeeded in restoring animation, and the perfect recovery of the boy, by means of his caresses, he induced the child to tie himself round his body. In this way he carried the poor little creature, as if in triumph, to the hospital.'

After his death the monks of St Bernard had Barry's body stuffed, and it now has a place of honour in the National Museum in Bern. The small bottle in which this legendary dog carried 'a reviving liquor for distressed travellers' still hangs from his neck.

A St Bernard is 100 times heavier than a chihuahua.

Dog Handling: A Point of Etiquette

If accompanied by a dog, or dogs, their owner must hold himself responsible for their good behaviour. If his pets trespass in any way he must apologise for them, and do his best to repair any damage they have done. Should one of his dogs jump on a lady and make her gown muddy, he must offer his services and endeavour to get rid of the traces of the accident, if the lady wishes. Should she show a disinclination to accept his aid, he must at once withdraw, raising his hat as he does so. Should his dog attack another dog he must immediately call him off, administer correction, and apologise to the owner of the dog assaulted. I saw a young man once, in these circumstances, beat the other dog, after his own had jumped on it and bitten its ear! He was dressed like a gentleman, but his behaviour gave a truer indication of him than did his garments.

Manners for Men by Mrs Humphry, 1897.

ONCE BITTEN

For years the most popular remedy for a dog bite was to apply a hair of the animal, always assuming you could catch it, to the wound. A variation of this was to get the victim to swallow some of the dog's hairs – or, better still, to eat a piece of its cooked liver.

As recently as 1866, it was reported at an inquest in the north of England that after a young girl had been bitten, the offending dog was killed and thrown into a river, then fished out again so that its liver could be extracted and fed to the child. Despite this 'infallible' antidote, the girl had died.

The idea that certain human diseases could be cured by transferring them to a dog was another widespread fallacy. Some of the patient's hair would be placed between slices of bread or meat and given to the dog to eat. The theory was that the animal absorbed the disease with the food, thus ridding the original sufferer of it. This panacea was used particularly to cure children's ailments such as whooping cough, measles and chicken pox.

Which probably accounts for there being so many spotted dogs around.

Suicide

An American gentleman possessing a valuable and intelligent bird-dog, purchased another dog, which he treated with great kindness, much to the disapproval of the old favourite. The signs of jealousy appeared more and more strongly and ended in what is believed to be a case of deliberate suicide. The dog was standing by a railroad track when a train approached, and as it was passing where the dog stood he sprang suddenly on the track between the front and rear wheels of a car and was instantly torn to pieces.

Pall Mall Gazette, 25 February 1884.

His Master's Voice

One of the most famous trademarks in the world is that of His Master's Voice: a dog listening to a gramophone. Yet it came about quite by chance.

One day in 1899 an artist named Francis Barraud called at the offices of The Gramophone Company in London and asked to borrow a brass horn. He explained that he had recently painted a picture of his dog Nipper – a small white mongrel – listening to a phonograph, but unfortunately nobody seemed interested in buying it. By changing the colour of the phonograph's large, horn-shaped speaker from black to brass, he hoped to liven up the picture and make it more attractive.

To demonstrate that he was serious, Barraud showed the painting, which he had titled 'His Master's Voice', to the company's general manager. The man was enchanted by it, and saw at once its commercial possibilities. Make the phonograph one of our modern gramophones, he told Barraud, and we will buy the painting from you. The price offered to the artist was £100, which included the purchase of the copyright. Barraud was delighted to accept.

In a matter of months, Nipper had made his mark on The Gramophone Company's products. He became a familiar figure in shop windows and 'starred' in all the advertising. His fame spread quickly throughout Europe, and then to New York where a giant rooftop hoarding of Nipper towered over the crowded pavements of Broadway.

But the little white dog never knew how famous he had become. He had died in 1895 – four years before the painting of 'His Master's Voice'.

LITTER PROBLEM

It is estimated that forty million American families
own at least one dog – and that another thousand
puppies are born every hour.

[Of dogs] It's the one species I wouldn't mind seeing vanish from
the face of the earth. I wish they were like the White Rhino –
six of them left in the Serengeti National Park, and all males.

Alan Bennett in *Getting On*

Dirty Dog

An officer in the Forty-fourth regiment who had occasion, when in Paris, to pass one of the bridges across the Seine, had his boots, which had been previously well polished, dirtied by a poodle dog rubbing against them. He in consequence went to a man who was stationed on the bridge, and had them cleaned. The same circumstance having occurred more than once, his curiosity was excited, and he watched the dog. He saw him roll himself in the mud of the river, and then watch for a person with well-polished boots, against which he contrived to rub himself. Finding that the shoe-black was the owner of the dog, he taxed him with the artifice; and after a little hesitation he confessed that he had taught the dog the trick in order to procure customers for himself. The officer, being much struck with the dog's sagacity, purchased him at a high price, and brought him to England. He kept him tied up in London some time, and then released him. The dog remained with him a day or two, and then made his escape. A fortnight afterwards he was found with his former master, pursuing his old trade on the bridge.

Edward Jesse, 1887

DOG WASH

An Italian inventor has developed an automatic washing-machine for dogs. The animal, who stands upright in the machine, is given a warm soapy wash, followed by a cold rinse and a hot blow-dry.
The dog-wash comes in three sizes – large, medium and small – and has a hole in the front through which the animal pokes its head.
That way it doesn't get soap in its eyes, water in its ears or hot air up its nose.

Dog Talk

The seventeenth-century German philosopher Gottfried
Leibniz reported to the French Academy that he had met and
examined a dog that could talk. The dog, which belonged to
a peasant farmer from Misnia, in Saxony, had a vocabulary
of some thirty words, and had been taught to speak by its
master. According to Leibniz, the animal would ask for its
food and drink, and could identify various other objects by
name. The French Academicians, on so eminent a testimony,
recorded the information as fact.

If dogs could talk, perhaps we would find it as hard to get
along with them as we do with people.

KAREL CAPEK

There was an old woman of York
Who tried teaching her dog to talk
After a week
It started to speak
And asked for a boneful of walk.

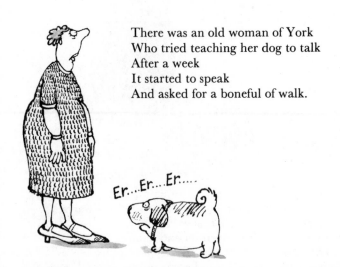

DOG LOVER EXTRAORDINAIRE

Of all the dog lovers throughout history few can have been more eccentric than Francis Henry Egerton, the immensely wealthy eighth Earl of Bridgewater (1756–1829). Not only were his dozen or so dogs transported everywhere by carriage in order to save their legs, but they also wore shoes, custom-made for them by his lordship's bootmaker.

Each day these cosseted canines would have dinner with their master. Seated at the table, with napkins round their necks, they would be waited on by servants – one to a dog. Generally, it is said, the animals behaved at the table with great decorum and restraint; but if one did happen to transgress any of the rules of good manners, he was swiftly punished. He would be banished to an ante-chamber, dressed in servant's livery, and forced to eat alone until the noble earl considered him sufficiently repentant.

I have always thought of a dog lover as a dog that was in love with another dog.

James Thurber

DO YOU TAKE THIS DOG?

That's a question which is being asked more and more these days in California, where canine weddings are becoming increasingly fashionable. For as little as $25 a preacher can be hired to bring together what, presumably, no dog may put asunder.

If the happy couple are lucky enough to have a honeymoon, then they can stay at one of California's pet hotels. A suite of their own, with fresh linen every day, specially prepared meals, a colour television and personal valet, will set their owners back around $70 a night. The price includes a daily check-up for the dogs by the resident vet.

If, despite all this, the marriage is soon heading for the rocks, help is always at hand in the form of therapy from a dog psychologist. This latest breed of medical practitioner specialises in curing the anxieties and neuroses of their four-legged patients. The average hour-long consultation costs between $30–40. For reasons that are all too clear, the psychologist often finds it rewarding to put the owner on the couch along with the dog.

A poodle who one day went punk
Shaved his crown as bald as a monk
Then he dyed his coat green
With mauve stripes in-between
And shampooed it with *eau de la skunk*.

POOPER SCOOPERS

'Pooper Scoopers' are all the rage in New York and other American cities where stiff fines are imposed on dog owners who let their animals foul public areas. These pickup devices range from disposable cardboard shovels to the long-handled 'Sooper Dooper Pooper Scooper', which allows you to clean up without bending over.

The latest product to hit the market is a scoop equipped with a flashlight, for operating after dark. It lightens the owner's load, as well as the dog's.

King Charles' Spaniels

Charles II took his fondness for spaniels to quite extraordinary lengths, as John Evelyn noted in his diary of 4 February 1685:

> He tooke delight in having a number of little spaniels follow him and lie in his bedchamber, where he often suffer'd the bitches to puppy and give suck, which render'd it very offensive, and indeede made the whole Court nasty and stinking.

Not surprisingly, the king was always very upset when one of his dogs was stolen, which seems to have happened quite often. The following advertisement, supposedly written by Charles himself, appeared in the *Mercurius Publicus* (28 June–5 July, 1660):

> We must call upon you again for a Black Dog between a greyhound, and a spaniel, no white about him, only a streak on his brest, and his tayl a little bobbed. It is His Majesties own Dog, and doubtless was stoln, for the dog was not born nor bred in England, and would never forsake His master. Whosoever findes him may acquaint any at Whitehal for the Dog was better known at Court, than those who stole him. Will they never leave robbing his Majesty! Must he not keep a Dog?

All I observed was the silliness of the king playing with his dogs all the while, and not minding the business.

SAMUEL PEPYS

YOUR MONEY OR YOUR DOG

Kidnapping dogs for ransom was a common practice in the nineteenth century. Dukes, bishops, ambassadors and other prominent people (and of course their dogs) regularly fell victim to unscrupulous thieves.

According to a House of Commons report on dog stealing, published in 1844, one thief 'extorted no less than £977.4s.6d. from the owners of dogs he had stolen and held to ransom'. A fortune in those days. On one occasion the Duke of Cambridge, youngest son of George III, was forced to pay £30 to get his animal back. And Elizabeth Browning wept 'for three days and nights' before handing over £50 in return for her beloved spaniel Flush.

STOCK-TAKING

In 1978, the last year in which such records
were kept, dogs in England and Wales killed
3951 sheep,
1760 poultry,
twelve pigs,
eleven cattle,
two goats,
and one horse.

When asked how to cure a dog of killing sheep,
Horace 'Go West, Young Man' Greeley advised:
'Cut off his tail behind the ears.'

The nose of the bulldog has been
slanted backwards so that he can breathe
without letting go.

WINSTON CHURCHILL

Don't Walk Under A Dog

Dogs figure prominently in the mythology and traditions of most countries, and there are countless superstitions about them even today.

In the Scottish Highlands, for example, a strange dog coming into a house heralds a new friendship; but one passing between a bridal couple on their wedding day is a bad omen.

In England, to come across a spotted or black-and-white dog while on the way to a business meeting is considered lucky; in India it means there is a disappointment in store.

In Lincolnshire, having met a white dog, you must remain silent until you have seen a white horse. That is, if you want to avoid bad luck. There will be good luck, however, if you chance upon three white dogs together.

For many fishermen it is courting disaster to utter the word 'dog' at sea. In some places this taboo extends to the animal itself, and the only sea-dogs allowed on board are two-legged ones.

Most people are agreed that a dog howling is bad news, if only because of the noise. In many parts of the world a lone dog howling at night is interpreted as a death omen, particularly if it happens in front of a house where someone lies ill. According to German folklore, if a dog looks downwards when it howls, it portends a death. If it looks upwards, some lucky person will recover from illness. A group of howling dogs in Poland means that an outbreak of plague is imminent.

But an old Staffordshire superstition could solve the problem for you: 'When you hear a dog howl, take off your shoe from the left foot and spit upon the sole. Place it on the ground, bottom upwards, and your foot upon the place you spat upon, which will not only preserve you from harm, but also stop the howling of the dog.'

FINGERS CROSSED

Beware of a silent dog and still water.

Latin proverb

A belligerent beagle named Hector
Bit the leg of a visiting rector
He then chewed an arm
Off a boy from the farm
And buried the refuse collector.

WHO NOSE?

There sprung a leak in Noah's ark,
Which made the dog begin to bark.
Noah took his nose to stop the hole,
And hence his nose is always cold.

Trad.

A dog's nose and a maid's knees are always cold.
English proverb

THE HIGHEST BIDDER

The wife of Sir Thomas More, Lord Chancellor of England during the reign of Henry VIII, was given a stray dog as a present. The dog had belonged previously to a beggarwoman who, when she discovered where it was, came to Sir Thomas to ask for the animal back, claiming that it had been stolen from her.

Sir Thomas was determined that justice should be done, despite his wife's obvious affection for the dog and desire to keep it. He instructed the beggarwoman to stand at one end of the long hall, and his wife at the other. Then, putting the dog down in the middle, he asked both women to call it. This they did, and without hesitation the animal ran to the beggarwoman.

The verdict was clear enough, but Lady More was so upset at losing her pet that Sir Thomas offered the beggarwoman a gold coin for it. The beggarwoman, delighted to receive so much money, willingly handed over the animal.

Thus Lady More, having lost the bidding, won the bid.

Money will buy a pretty good dog, but it won't buy the wag of his tail.

Josh Billings

WATCH-DOG

In 1954, a collie which had kept a fifteen-week
vigil beside the dead body of its master was
given a medal by the National Canine
Defence League. The dog's owner, a shepherd,
had disappeared on the Yorkshire moors
during the winter. When over three months
later his body was found, the dog, weak from
hunger and hardly able to walk, was still
guarding him.

Underdogs

I have all my life had a sympathy for mongrel,
ungainly dogs, who are nobody's pets; and I
would rather surprise one of them by a pat and a
pleasant morsel, than meet the condescending
advances of the loveliest Skye terrier who has his
cushion by my lady's chair.

George Eliot (Scenes of Clerical Life)

BEDTIME STORY

In a barrack room in the south of England, an officer found his dog lying on his bed, and gave him a severe flogging. Next day he discovered the dog in the act of jumping off the bed, and again gave him a sound thrashing. The day following the dog was not actually upon the bed, but his master found a warm place thereon, on which the animal had evidently been reposing, and he was castigated for a third time. On the fourth day, as the officer opened his bedroom door, he found the dog with his paws on the bed, in the act of blowing the place on which he had been lying, in order to cool it.

Nineteenth-century anecdote

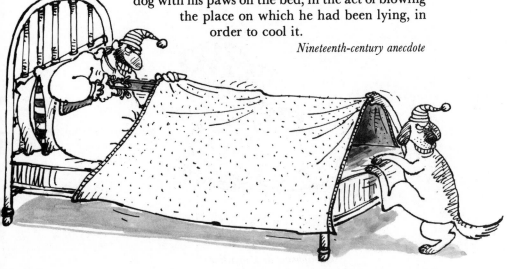

**Whenever a man is lonely,
God sends him a dog.**

Alphonse de Lamartine